Sounds All Around Us

Different Sounds

Charlotte Guillain

Heinemann Library
Chicago, Illinois

www.heinemannraintree.com
Visit our website to find out more information about Heinemann-Raintree books.

To order:
☎ Phone 888-454-2279
💻 Visit www.heinemannraintree.com to browse our catalog and order online.

Designed by Joanna Hinton-Malivoire
Photo research by Tracy Cummins and Tracey Engel
Printed and bound by South China Printing Company Ltd

13 12 11 10 09
10 9 8 7 6 5 4 3 2 1

Library of Congress Cataloging-in-Publication Data
Guillain, Charlotte.
Different sounds / Charlotte Guillain.
p. cm. -- (Sounds around us)
Includes bibliographical references and index.
ISBN 978-1-4329-3202-2 (hc) -- ISBN 978-1-4329-3208-4 (pb)
1. Sound--Juvenile literature. 2. Sound-waves--Juvenile literature. I. Title.
QC225.5.G8496 2008
534--dc22
2008051740

Acknowledgments
The author and publishers are grateful to the following for permission to reproduce copyright material: Alamy pp. **4 top left** (©UpperCut Images), **6** (©Ted Pink), **13** (©Derek Croucher), **15** (©JUPITER IMAGES/Polka Dot), **19** (©PCL), **20** (©Alan Myers), **21** (©anna Sherwin), **23a** (©anna Sherwin), **23c** (©Ted Pink); Getty Images pp. **5** (©Donald Miralle), **7** (©Lester Lefkowitz), **10** (©Holger Leue), **11** (©AFP/BORIS HORVAT), **18** (©Niki Mareschal), **23b** (©Lester Lefkowitz); iStockphoto pp. **4 top right** (©Frank Leung), **4 bottom right** (©Peeter Viisimaa); Jupiter Images p. **14** (©Image Ideas); NASA p. **8** (©GRIN); Photolibrary pp. **12** (©David & Micha Sheldon), **16** (©Index Stock Imagery), **17** (©Picture Press/Manfred Delpho); Shutterstock pp. **4 bottom left** (©devi), **9** (©Amra Pasic).

Cover photograph of Silk Road, China reproduced with permission of Getty Images (©Keren Su). Back cover photograph of some teenage girls playing flutes reproduced with permission of Alamy (©Jupiter Images/Polka Dot).

The publishers would like to thank Nancy Harris and Adriana Scalise for their assistance in the preparation of this book.

Every effort has been made to contact copyright holders of any material reproduced in this book. Any omissions will be rectified in subsequent printings if notice is given to the publisher.

Contents

Sounds

There are many different sounds.

We hear different sounds around us
every day.

Sound Waves

Sounds make the air shake,
or vibrate.

sound wave

When the air vibrates, it is called a
sound wave.

Loud and Quiet Sounds

Some sounds are loud.

Big sound waves make loud sounds.

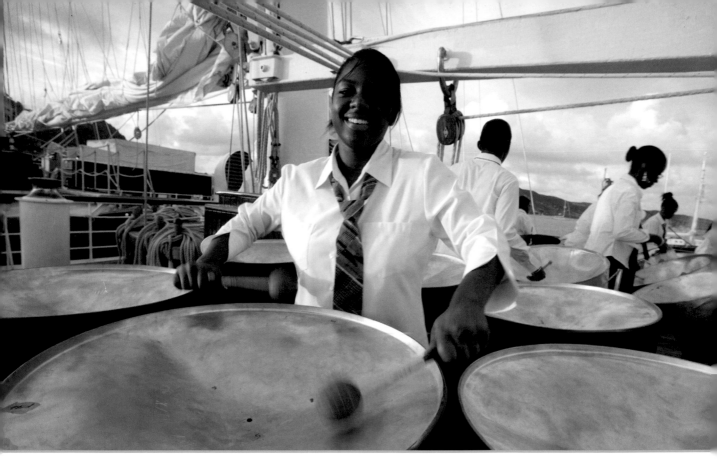

A drum can make loud sounds.

A trumpet can make loud sounds.

Some sounds are quiet.

Small sound waves make
quiet sounds.

A harp can make quiet sounds.

A flute can make quiet sounds.

High and Low Sounds

Some sounds are high.

Very fast sound waves make
high sounds.

Some sounds are low.

Very slow sound waves make
low sounds.

A triangle can make high sounds.

A double bass can make low sounds.

What Have You Learned?

- Big sound waves make loud sounds.

- Small sound waves make quiet sounds.

- Very fast sound waves make high sounds.

- Very slow sound waves make low sounds.

Picture Glossary

double bass musical instrument that looks like a large violin

sound wave when the air shakes very quickly

vibrate shake very quickly

Index

Note to Parents and Teachers
Before reading
Tell children that sounds can be loud or quiet, high or low. Explain that big sound waves make loud sounds, and small sound waves make quiet sounds. Also explain that if sound waves are fast, they make high sounds, and if sound waves are slow, they make low sounds.

After reading
• Give children a box filled with a variety of objects, such as a harmonica, a drum, bells, a bouncy ball, a whistle, a rattle, and anything else you can think of. Ask the children to make predictions about the types of sounds the objects will make. Tell the children to shake, blow, or bang the objects to make different sounds.